BIG IDEA

&

THE NATURE TRAIL

A GOOD OLD BOY'S
TAO TE CHING

James Tucker - "The Old Geezer"

FORWARD DRAWKCAB

This book is a reflection of my trail ridings with Clarence Jordan and Gia-fu Feng.

1970's – A personal crisis transformed me from a teenage smart aleck atheist, into a twenty-something street corner preacher. Clarence Jordan's "Cotton Patch Gospels" was a pivotal guide book that helped me find my way. Jordan was a Southern Baptist and a Greek scholar who also founded Koinonia Farms, the birthplace of Habitat for Humanity. His colloquial translation of the New Testament stories of Jesus helped me to see the gospel on my on terms in the country characters and vernacular of my Southern heritage. I considered him a mentor but I never had the pleasure of meeting Clarence Jordan.

1980's – The second big book of my young adulthood was Gia-fu Feng's translation of the "Tao Te Ching", perhaps the second most translated spiritual text in history. It is a beautiful coffee table book illustrated with black and white photography, Gia-fu's Chinese calligraphy and his poetic English translation of Lao Tse's eighty-one chapters.

I kept Gia-Fu's book on my coffee table and pondered my way through Lao Tse's take on things ineffable. Once again, crisis moved me. I sold my car, bought a Greyhound bus ticket, and showed up at Gia-fu's commune in the Rocky Mountains. I was broke, had no return ticket, and was an odd Southerner in the midst of mostly European Tai Chi students, monks, spiritual seekers and groovy trippers. Gia-Fu took me in on his scholarship program and for the next couple of years I moved between the Stillpoint commune in the forest and his big house above the Pikes Peak COG Railroad station in Manitou Springs, Colorado.

Stillpoint is dotted with tiny isolated hermitage cabins spread across the hillsides, nestled into the Wet Mountains of Colorado. After each day's assigned activities, in late afternoon, residents would retire alone to our cabins for private meditation, reading, journaling; all the sorts of things one does in a 10'x10' cabin adorned with little more than a sleeping bag. All the hermits had their own windup alarm clocks to wake us around 2:00 am. We would gather together near the dirt road entrance to Stillpoint in a big recycled mobile home which served as the kitchen, bath house and meeting room for the commune. After a few hours of meditation, baths, hot tea and shelling peanuts, Gia-fu would show up and begin lecturing just before dawn. It was the most fun and enlightening part of our day.

Gia-Fu called himself "the Bob Hope of consciousness".

In October of 1983, Gia-fu shifted his morning lessons into a group retranslation exercise and we set about revising all 81 chapters of the Tao Te Ching. The notion of reinterpreting those chapters in the fashion of Clarence Jordan's "Cotton Patch Gospels" came to me that month.

It has taken thirty years of cogitating to bring forth the inspiration I received from those two good old boys.

This is it!

Jimmy Tucker, aka Geezer – April 20, 2015

Stillpoint over the years

TAI CHI CHÚAN

Jimmy & Laurie - 2009

ACKNOWLEDGMENTS

It takes a certain kind of jackass to keep on talking
after the first thing he says is that nothing can be said.

ONE

If ya'll can wrap yer' heads around it,
it ain't the Big Idea.

And the Nature Trail won't fit on a map
any more than the Big Idea
can squeeze into yer' noggin.

Yet, all the little notions
sprang from the Big Idea
and bequeathed us the best stories
along the Nature Trail.

Let the wild things roam free.

If you crave to corral 'em,
you'll just harness yer' own self.

Big Idea and the Nature Trail
can't be understood.

But cogitating on 'em
just might keep you from getting lost.

all the little notions
sprang from the Big Idea

and bequeathed us the best stories
along the Nature Trail

TWO

If you want to call a square jawed hero handsome,
you need an ugly scar-faced villain
to put up against him.

We only recognize the good guys
'cause of our encounters with the bad guys,
and vice versa.

Hard workers and lazy bums,
sour lemons and sweet candy,
high mountains and deep valleys,
song birds and screeching crows,
heads and tails.

It is the contrast,
the two sides of a coin
that gives us perspective.

So a good old boy
will mosey along without making a fuss.

His trail will have rainy days and clear skies,
successes and failures, joys and sorrows.

In the end everything will work out
just as it should,
and the good old boy
will have no need to take credit for any of it.

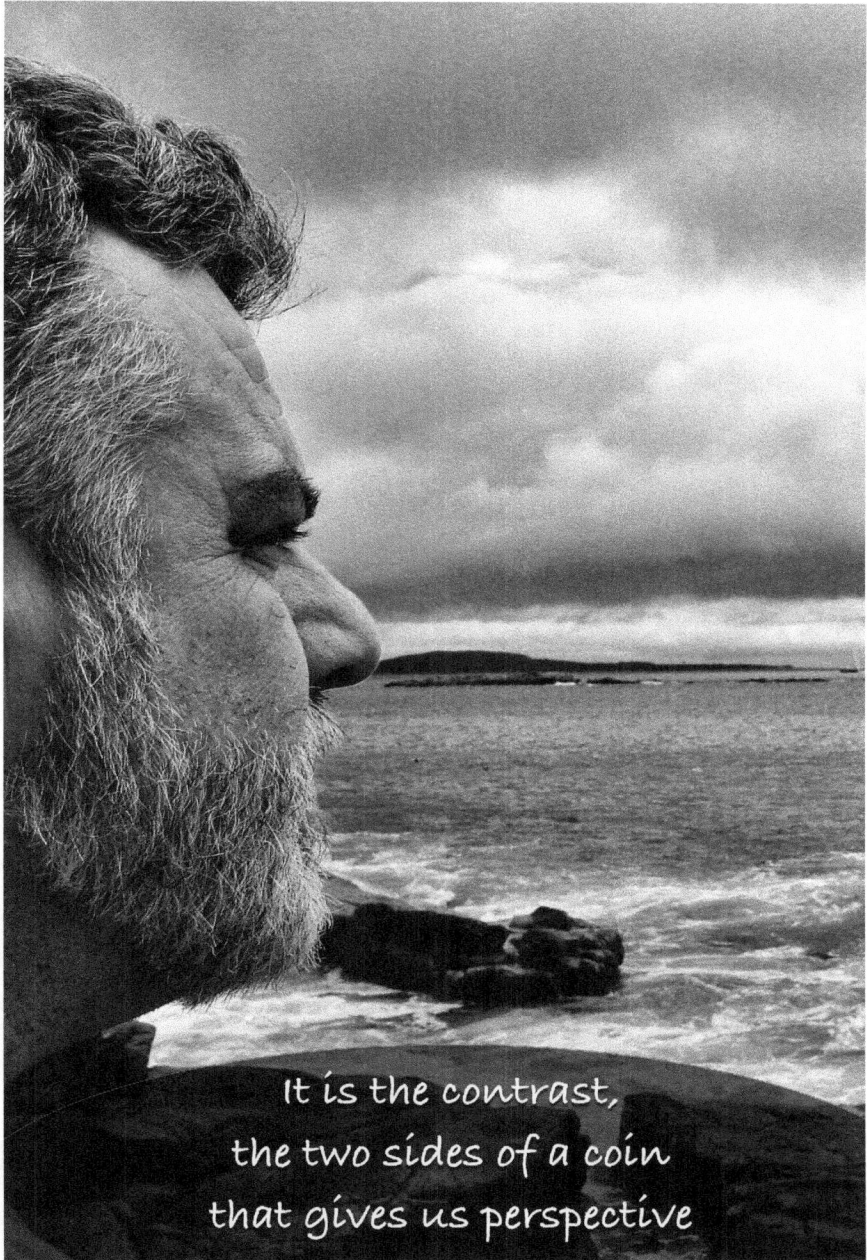

It is the contrast,
the two sides of a coin
that gives us perspective

THREE

Don't brag about yer' good deeds
and no one will think you are a braggart.

Don't pile up expensive stuff,
and no one will want to steal your stuff.

A good old boy
don't point out to folks
the things they don't have.

He helps them appreciate
what they've got.

He don't spin tales
about places and things
that cause yearnings in their hearts.

He helps his neighbors be content,
'cause he is satisfied in his own self.

FOUR

The Big Idea
seems to be nonsense,
but it makes perfect sense
out of the whole dang
kit and caboodle.

Give it a little thought
and yer' mouth will drop open,
yer' eyes will glaze over.

Go on thinking 'bout it
and yer' pokey points will smooth out,
yer' tangled knots will come loose.

My, my, my.

It's bigger than big
and sits stiller
than a granite mountain.

Ain't got a clue where it came from.

I reckon it was the grand-pappy of the Lord.

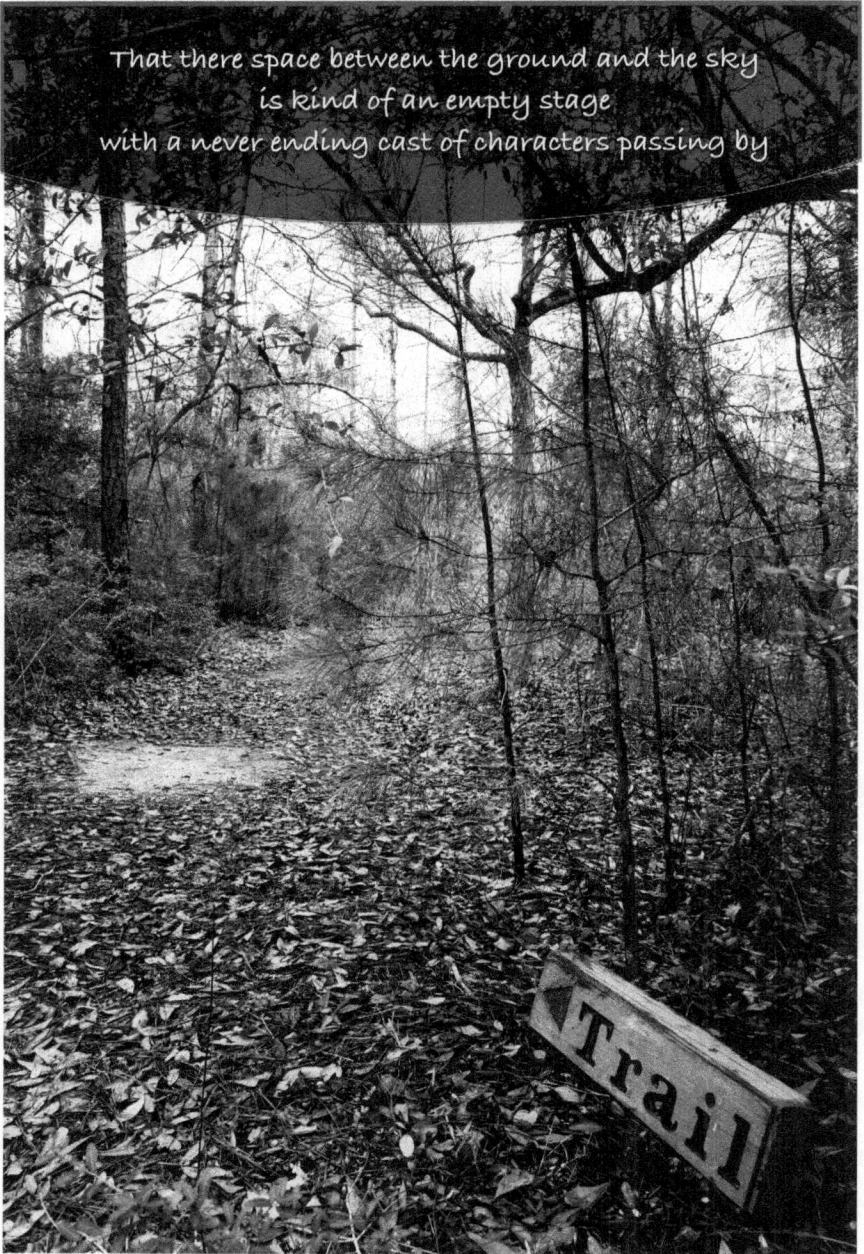

That there space between the ground and the sky
is kind of an empty stage
with a never ending cast of characters passing by

FIVE

The ground and sky
don't play favorites.

Every fella gets to
suck in all the air he wants.

At the end of the trail
a pine box is buried
in the same ground
as a copper casket.

That there space between
the ground and the sky
is kind of an empty stage
with a never ending cast
of characters passing by.

So ya'll don't pay too much attention
to the tattle-tale tongue waggers.

They'll talk themselves out soon enough.

SIX

A peaceful valley is like
the undying love of yer' mother.

No one can explain
this nurturing source.

From the spirit of woman
all good things are renewed
without consternation.

SEVEN

The sky and the ground don't run out.

They was here for my grand-pappy
and they'll be here after I'm gone.

How come they don't get used up?
'Cause they ain't here
fer their own selves!

That's why a good old boy
don't push to the front of the line.

He lets other folk go first.

Everybody appreciates that,
and he always ends up
with a good seat anyhow.

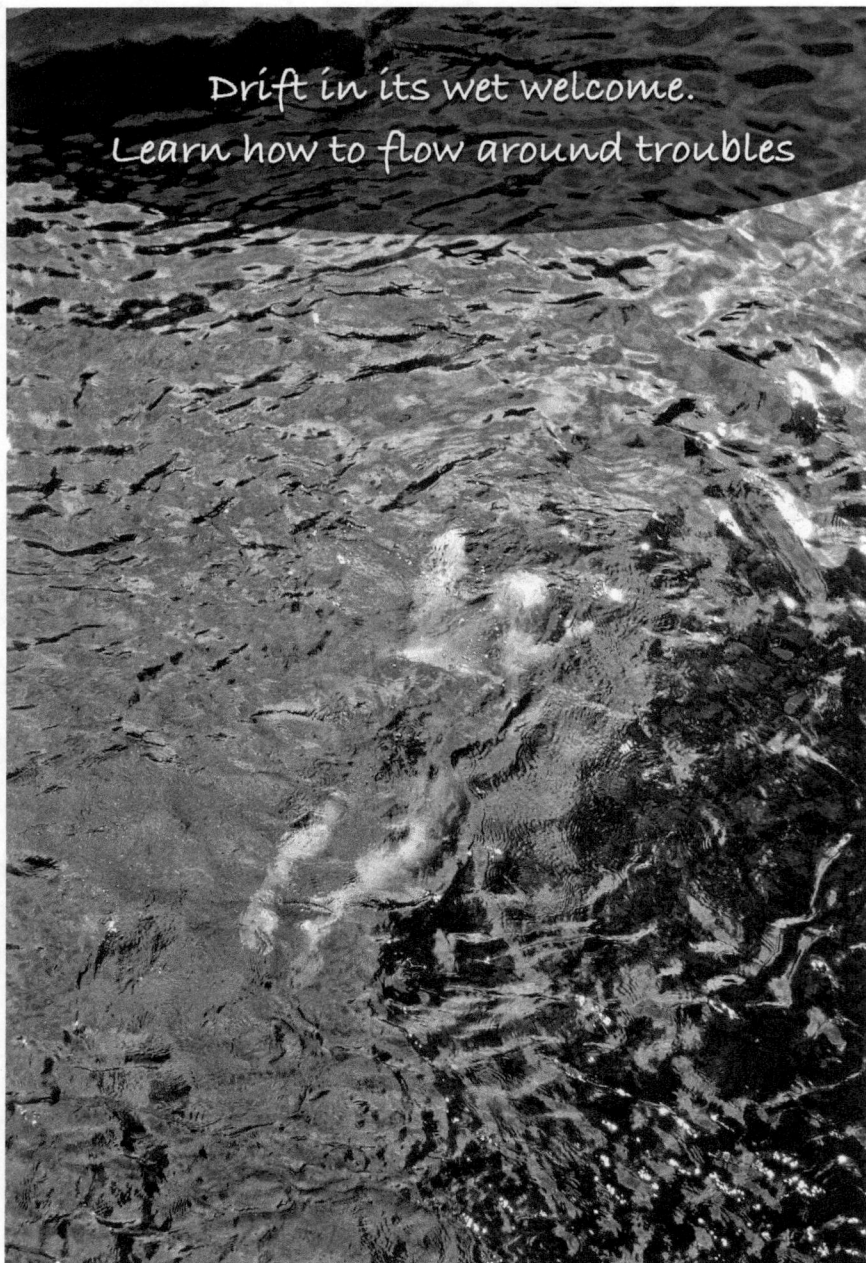

Drift in its wet welcome.
Learn how to flow around troubles

EIGHT

If ya'll want to get a better handle
on the Big Idea.

Dive in to the swimming hole.

The water will say,
"come on in"
to any good old boy
who wants to take the plunge.

Cool and soothing
with a gentle current
that turns mountains
into valleys
in its own time.

Drift in its wet welcome.

Learn how to flow around troubles
and fill life to the brim
with a double dip of generosity.

After you win the rodeo,
head on back to the ranch

NINE

Don't waste water
trying to fill a canteen
that is already full.

And if you keep on
'a sharpening a knife
that already has a good edge,
pretty soon you'll be left with
nothin' but a knife handle.

If you leave your best saddle
and pearl handled revolver
in an unguarded bunk house.

You can be sure
that some scallywag
will make off with 'em.

After you win the rodeo,
head on back to the ranch.

A good old boy
don't need to stick around
for all the backslapping commotion.

TEN

A seasoned ranch hand
keeps his eye on the herd
and his noggin don't drift.

He has a gentle get-along with the strays
when he leads 'em back in.

And he trusts his trail boss
to find the best way across the bad lands.

A good trail boss
is as easy with his wranglers
as they are with the herd.

He don't need to bark orders.

He makes sure
there is plenty of good grub
when the work is done.

And if the owner
gives a bonus at the end of the drive,
he passes it on to his cowpokes.

That's why he is called
the best of the good old boys.

A good trail boss
is as easy with his wranglers
as they are with the herd

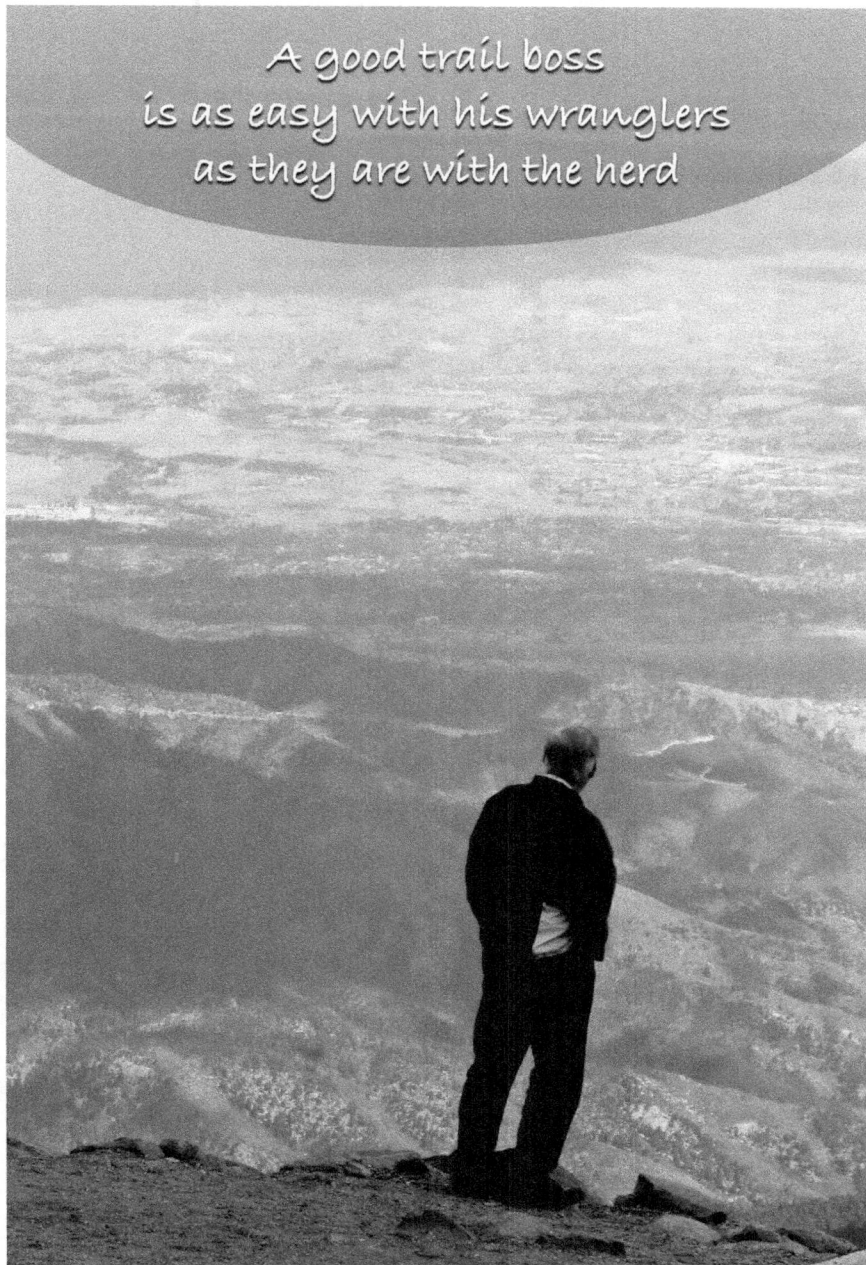

ELEVEN

It don't matter how many spokes
you have on your wagon wheel
if there ain't a hole in the middle
for your axle.

It's that empty hole
that makes the wheel useful.

Just the same,
it's the inside of the cup
where you pour your coffee.

And you value a roof over your head
'cause there is empty space under that roof
where you can live.

Pretty much every thing that gets made
is only worth something
'cause it shapes a receptive space.

This is true for your heart and noggin too.

every thing that gets made
is only worth something
'cause it shapes a receptive space

TWELVE

When it's too bright,
you can't see.

Too noisy
and you can't make sense
of what you hear.

Too much
salt and pepper
will ruin your dinner.

Too much
horse racing, hunting and fishing,
spoils the fun
and makes you
pretty much worthless.

So a good old boy
will be quiet, cogitate, rest his noggin
and fergit about all that foolishness.

THIRTEEN

A good old boy
don't think anymore of
a slap on the back
than he does
a kick in the seat of his pants.

Now why do you think that is?

When you get put up on a pedestal,
pretty soon yer' all outta kilter
worrying about falling off.

So don't waste time
fussin' about yer' own self.

Take care of the herd
like it's yer' own self.

That's what'll make for happy trails.

FOURTEEN

Sometimes out on the prairie,
a fella will peer at the horizon,
not quite sure of what he can't see.

And in the still of the night,
he will listen for a sound that ain't there.

The Big Idea is kinda like that.

You look for it and you can't find it.

Listen and you can't hear it.

Grab for it
and there is not even anything there
to slip through your fingers.

Yet, somehow a good old boy
will hold tight to the Big Idea
and it will lead him on down the Nature Trail.

This is a secret that nobody can tell you.

You just gotta figger it out fer yer' self.

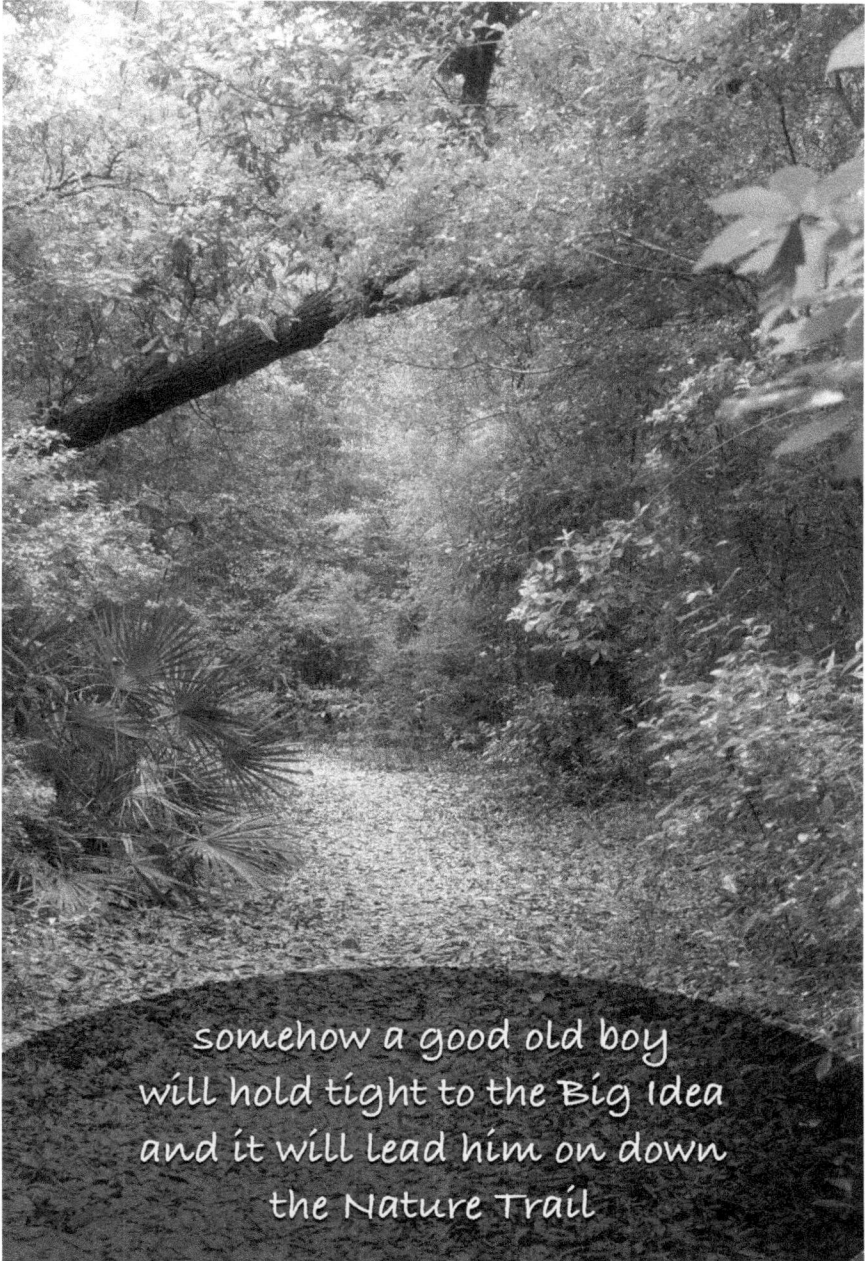

somehow a good old boy
will hold tight to the Big Idea
and it will lead him on down
the Nature Trail

FIFTEEN

The best of the good old boys
could tell you a lot
without saying a word.

Since they didn't waste time
yammering on about what they knew,
all I can do is try to describe them.

They was careful fellas,
you never saw them
trying to take the herd across the river
at a tricky spot.

If they came up on a stranger,
they'd treat him with good manners,
like a neighbor,
but they'd never let a stranger
get the drop on them.

When the swimming hole
was muddy,
the good old boys
would just rest on the bank
and let the water clear up
before they dove in.

They were never in a hurry
and they never acted like greenhorns.

SIXTEEN

When a good old boy is sitting quiet
with nothing on his mind,
he ain't empty headed.

He is just watching the plants bloom
and the critters scurrying about,
doing what comes natural.

Roots push out trees
which make pretty leaves
that fall back on the ground
and mulch into dirt
to feed the roots.

Critters move through life and death
in a similar circle.

So when a good old boy withers
and gets cricky in his bones,
he don't fret at all.

He has seen the way of all things
and knows it is his destiny
to push up daisies on the Nature Trail.

In the best run outfits
the owner of the herd and the
wranglers never even think
about the trail boss

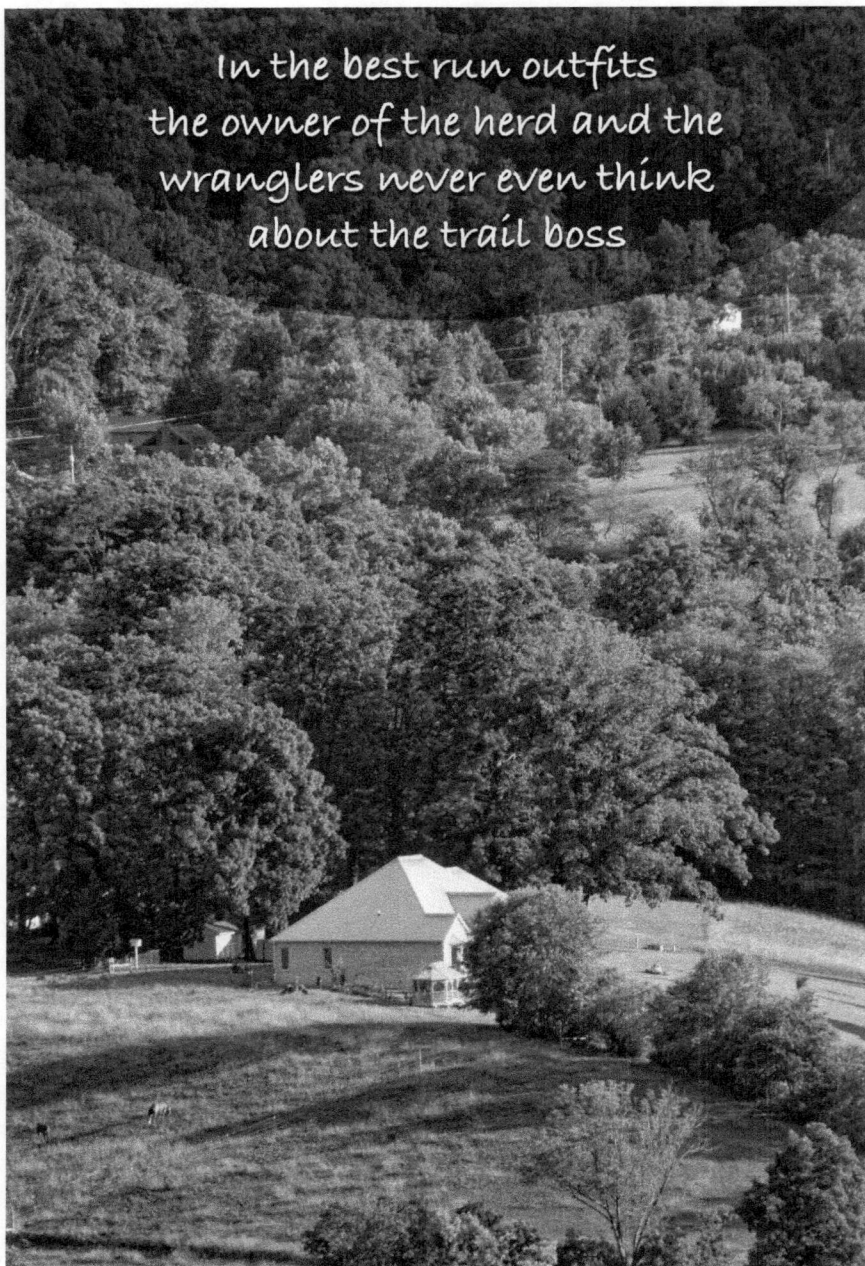

SEVENTEEN

In the best run outfits
the owner of the herd and the wranglers
never even think about the trail boss.

In the second tier of ranches,
the trail boss is loved and praised.

You know you've really
moved down the pecking order
when you find an outfit
where the trail boss is feared,
or worse yet, cussed behind his back.

When the best of the good old boys
is running the show,
the cattle drive goes smooth,
the work gets done,
and the wranglers think
they made it all happen
their own selves.

Which is just how
the trail boss planned it.

EIGHTEEN

When the Big Idea is forgotten.

Do-gooders and glad-handers
come around.

Smarty pants and tricky Dicks
will show their two faces.

Yer' kin will act like strangers
and nary a soul will remember
that blood is thicker than water.

NINETEEN

Give up on being a do-gooder,
quit trying to figure everything out,
and it will be a whole lot better for everybody.

Don't act like Mister Nice Guy goody-two-shoes
and your kin will remember
that they is connected by blood and heart.

Quit yer' clever quick buck chasing
and the bandits won't have no reason to rob you.

Now those three pieces of advice
are just about how things appear
to folks along the trail.

What they can't see is more important.

If you want to be a good old boy,
just keep it simple,
stay true to yer' own self,
be willing to share
and control yer' inner cravings.

Like a newborn critter just
opening his eyes on the prairie,
he is alone and has no place to go

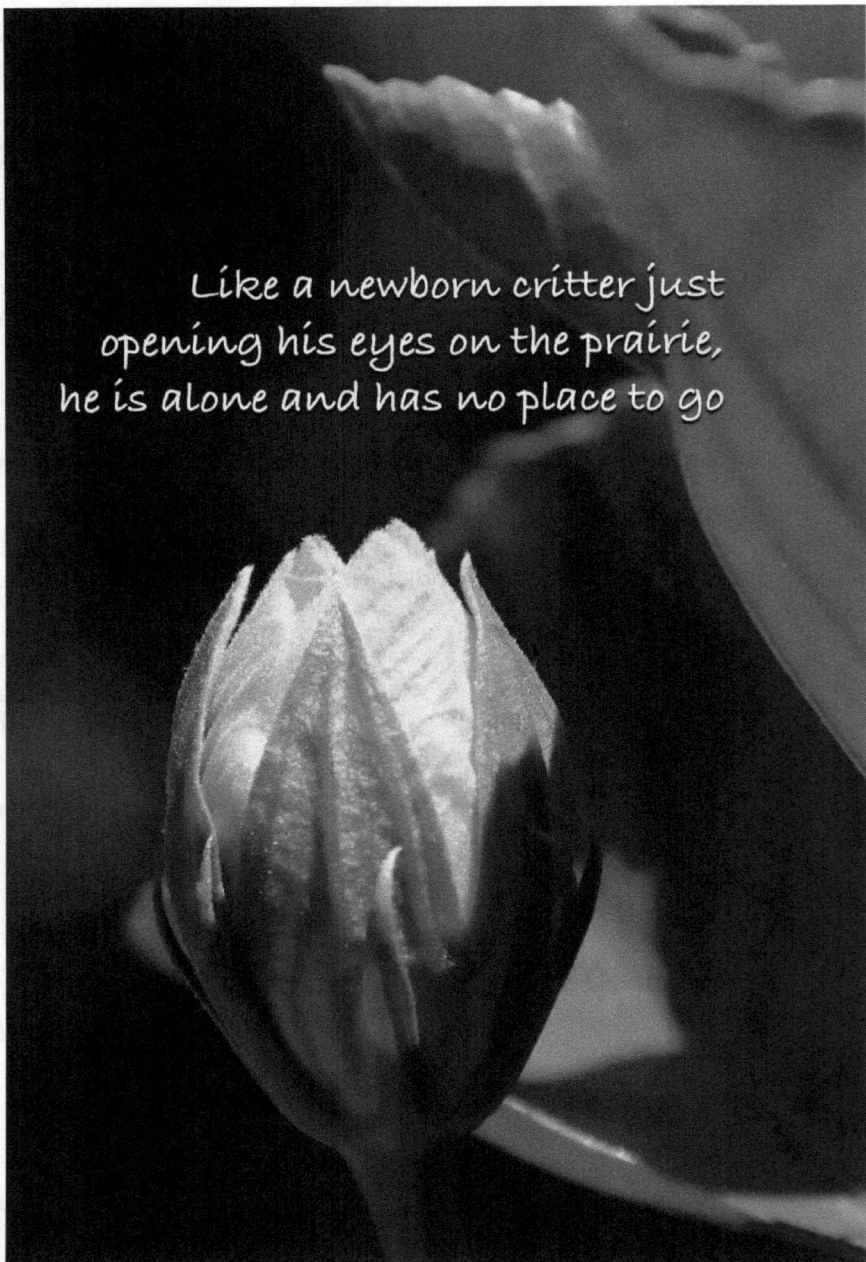

TWENTY

If you don't want to get knocked around,
drop outta the school of hard knocks.

It ain't taught you the difference 'tween yep and nope,
nor who's the good guys, nor who's the bad guys.

Think I'm afraid of what scares the city folk?
Balderdash!

City folk are just stuck in their tea parties.
They think going to the park and sitting on a bench is getting outside.
A good old boy tumbles like a tumbleweed,
not caring where the wind blows.

Like a newborn critter just opening his eyes on the prairie,
he is alone and has no place to go.

Cityfolk have more than they need.
I ain't got a dadgum thing.
I'm a fool. Yes-sir-ree, I am discombobulated.

Cityfolk are sharp and slick, but I am dull and rough.
Oh, my, my! I am a homeless drifter.
Coming from nowhere, going to nowhere.

Cityfolk are always getting together
and got something to do.
Me, I'm all alone. Got no agendas.
Got nothing to get excited about.

I ain't like them.
I live off the land
and mother earth takes care of me.

TWENTYONE

The very best thing
is to go where
the Big Idea leads you.

The Trail is winding and hard to follow.

Oh winding and hard to follow,
but it is a way.

Oh hard to follow and winding,
but it is its own destination.

Oh it is hard to see,
yet it is your Trail.

You know it is your Trail
because you are following your heart.

From my grand-pappy's day
'til I passed it on to you,
the way has never been lost.

This is how I see the Nature Trail.

Why do I follow the Big Idea?

Because of this...

TWENTYTWO

What seems to be parts and pieces
will turn out to be the whole enchilada.

The road that looks like it is snaking to nowhere
will take you home straight away.

An empty canteen can quench your thirst.

A worn out old hoss can gallop like a new pony.

The fella who doesn't want much will get his fill.

And the grub greedy will go hungry.

So the good old boy avoids the lime light
and watches out for the whole herd.

He doesn't show off
and his accomplishments are always noticed.

He never pushes to the head of the pack,
so the whole outfit is always happy to follow him.

Yes-sir-ree! Like my grandpappy always said;

"Don't let yer' self think yer' lacking
and you'll always have plenty"

TWENTYTHREE

A good old boy
don't waste words.

Even when it is raining a gully washer
and blowing like a hurricane,
it will be clear and calm after a spell.

So if the weather can't get stuck in a rut,
how can any fella be always constant?

Go on about your business
with the Big Idea in mind
and folk will say
you remind them of the Big Idea.

Put one foot after the other
down the Nature Trail
and folk will follow you.

Remember the Big Idea
and the Big Idea will remember you.

Find your way on the Nature Trail
and the Trail will not fail you.

Fill your head with nonsense and gallivant around
and you will become muddled and lost.

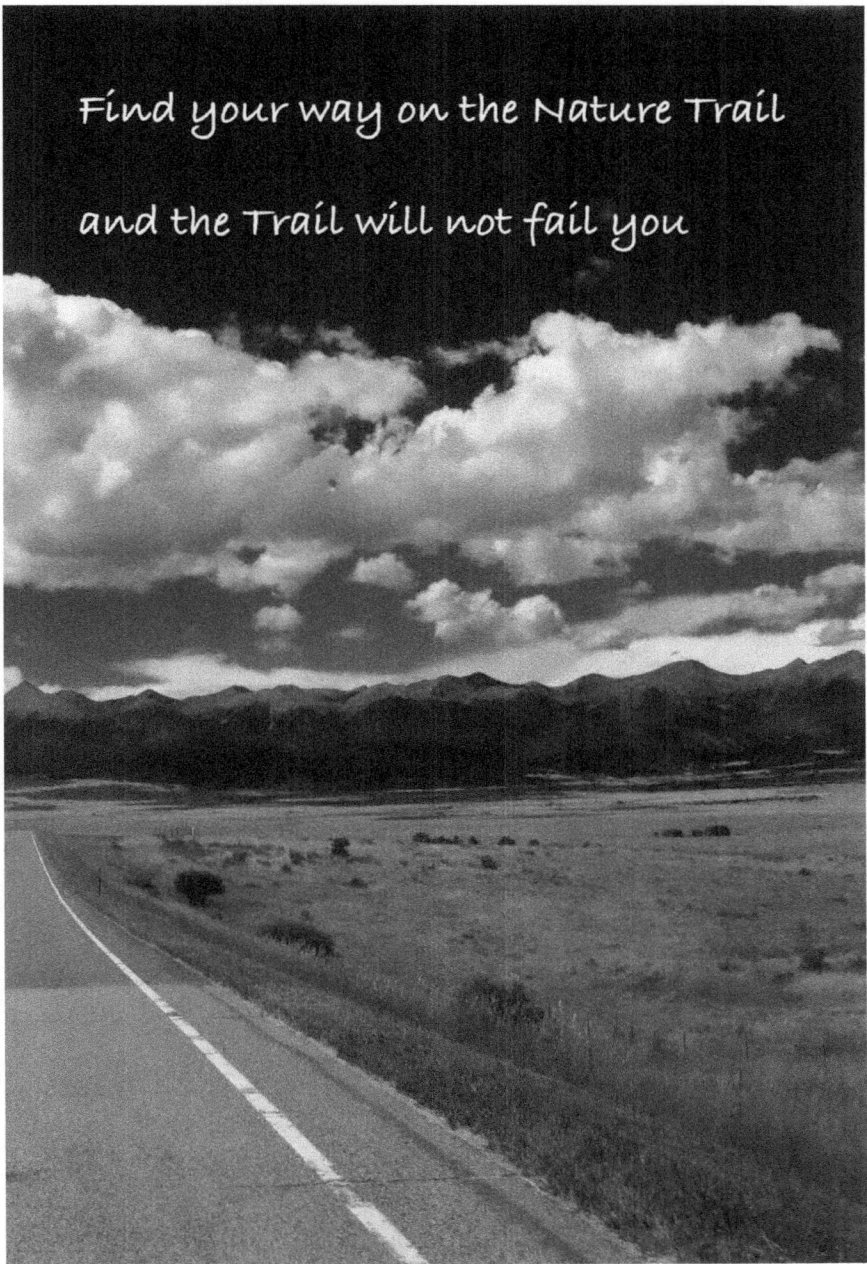

Find your way on the Nature Trail

and the Trail will not fail you

TWENTYFOUR

A fella up on his tippy toes
will wobble for sure

He says he is going to stretch his legs
but he stays stuck in the same spot

Self promoters
don't have anything worth promoting

Self asserters
are nothing but ordinary

And when they start
singing their own praises,
you can be sure it is a tune to forget.

Fellas who indulge in such behaviors
don't know the difference
between a cow patty
and a buttermilk pancake.

A good old boy
has no time for such foolishness.

TWENTYFIVE

T'was before heaven and earth.

Still, void and formless

Yet it was unchanging and inexhaustible

A canvas for heaven and earth

It is too big and far reaching
for my little pea brain to give it a name

If you insist,
I'll just call it, The Big Idea

However far and long you travel,
you will find the Big Idea
at the end of your trail.

And when you get back to the ranch,
you'll discover that the Big Idea never left.

Man comes from the dust of the earth,
earth comes from the dust of heaven,
the heavens sprang from the Big Idea
and the Big Idea is its own big idea.

Nothing will agitate
his quiet mind
or cause him to loose focus
on what's before him

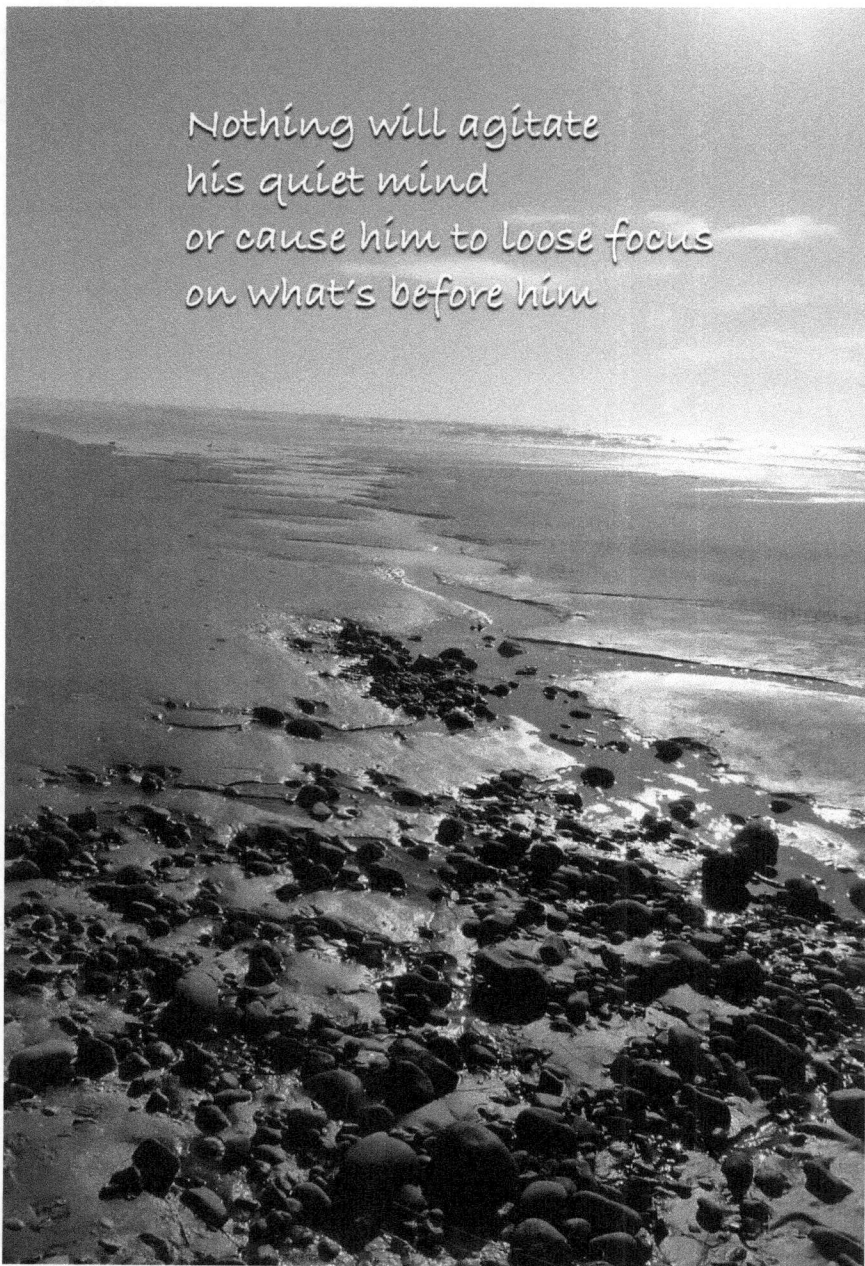

TWENTYSIX

If you've never hauled a heavy load
you can't appreciate a light load.

If you've never hunkered down and sat still
you won't have much perspective on
"quick, lickety-split".

So a good old boy
will stay steady in the saddle
all day down the trail.

He won't get worked up over
magnificent mountains
and beautiful sunsets,
nor fret over
storm clouds or bear tracks.

Nothing will agitate
his quiet mind
or cause him to loose focus
on what's before him.

The owner of the herd should
learn this lesson from the good old boy
or else he will become bum-fuzzled
and lose the respect of his ranch hands
then see his cattle become dry bones.

TWENTYSEVEN

The best tracker won't leave tracks.

The best talker won't get tongue tied.

The best tally man won't loose count.

The best locksmith won't get picked.

The best roper won't loose his noose.

A good old boy is good to all men,
straight shooters and scalawags alike.

He sees no one as worthless
and brings out the best
in everyone on the roundup
without anyone seeing how he does it.

This is why the good old boy
is known as the scoundrel's teacher,
and how the scoundrel
becomes a worthy helper.

Now, this will discombobulate
old Mr. Smartypants
'cause he just can't understand
how the good old boy stays steady and true
on the nature trail.

A good old boy
is good to all men,
straight shooters
and scalawags alike

TWENTYEIGHT

Know yer strength
and yer weakness.

Be receptive
to the flow of life.

Embrace the years
and be young again.

Don't fear
the darkness in you
and your light
will never cease to shine.

Don't glory in your greatness
nor wallow in your shame.

Open yer heart
and be receptive
to what life brings
and yer heart
will be a source
for what the world needs.

Keep yer focus simple
and the little you have
will be more than enough
for those who ask you to lead.

TWENTYNINE

A wrangler who tries
to fence in the sky and prairie
will show himself to be a silly fool.

The sky and prairie are like the big idea.

You can't corral it without spoiling what you touch.

Grab on to it fer yer self
and you will just have empty hands.

In the course of things
there are leaders and followers,
dusty cowpokes and city dandies,
muscle heads and milk toasts,
winners and losers.

That's why the good old boy
always moseys easy,
keeps things simple
and never over indulges.

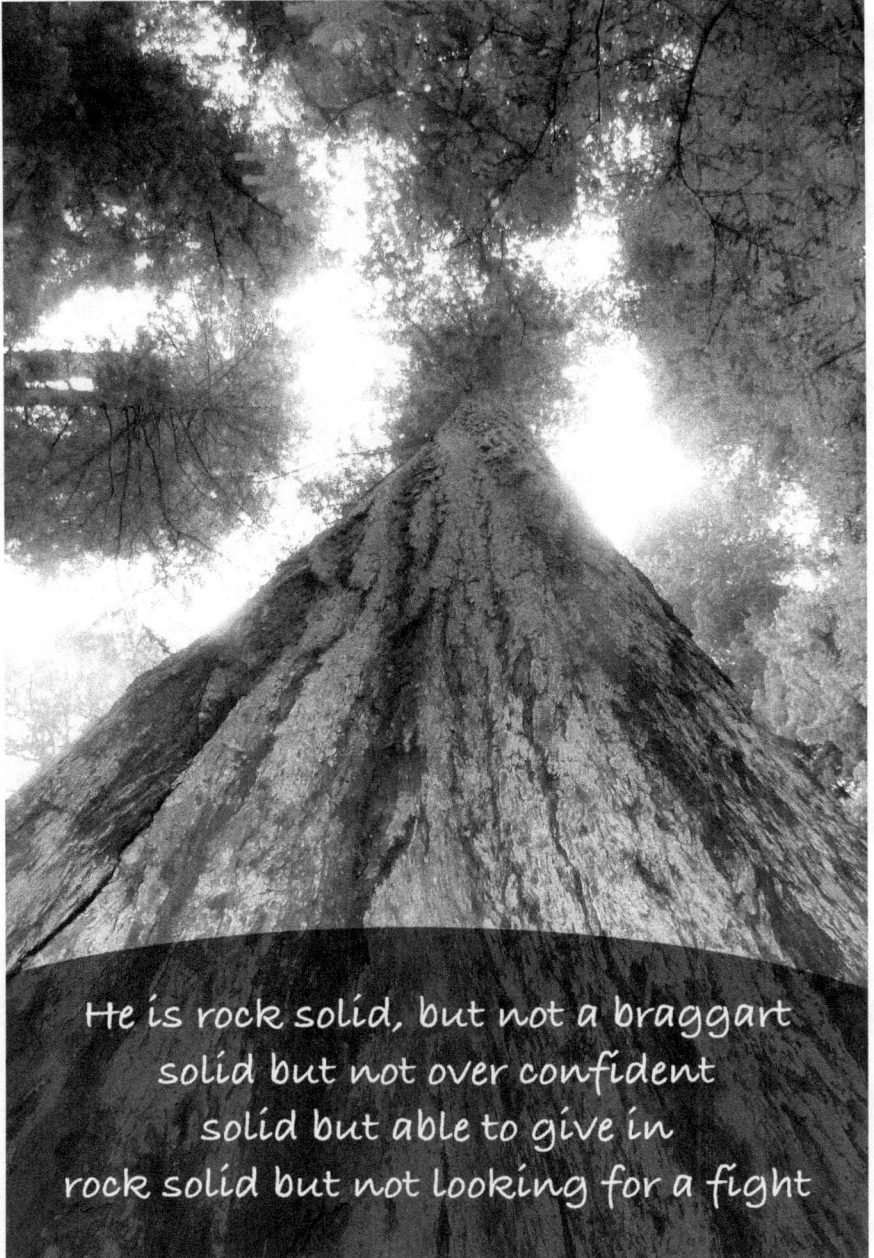

He is rock solid, but not a braggart
solid but not over confident
solid but able to give in
rock solid but not looking for a fight

THIRTY

A good old boy
is able to help out
the owner of the herd
'cause his inclination
is to avoid conflagration.

When trouble comes and he has to act,
he knows that fighting will endanger the herd.

He does what is necessary and no more.

He is rock solid,
but not a braggart,
solid but not over confident,
solid but able to give in,
rock solid
but not looking for a fight.

It might seem like
winning a fight
will get you ahead,
but fighting is
contrary to the big idea
and will end up
making you a loser every time.

THIRTYONE

Some fellas like the sight
of a shotgun, a rifle or a six shooter.

But a good old boy knows better.

Guns are tools for death
and best avoided if at all possible.

Better the open left hand of peaceful greeting
than the cold right hand of lead justice.

The good old boy seeks peace and quiet
and freedom from grudges.

If'n he has to fight,
he takes no pleasure in it,
he never celebrates his victories.

A wrangler who takes pleasure in killing
will never be a trusted leader on the trail.

A good old boy treasures his happy time
back at the ranch
where he doesn't wear his gun belt.

And when he is forced to fight,
it fills him with sorrow
'cause he knows it will
lead to somebody's funeral.

THIRTYTWO

The Big Idea can not be named,
even if I call it the big idea.

Call me simple minded,
but I just can't wrap my head around it
and neither can you nor anybody else.

It is too small
and too big
we can't keep it in
and we can't let it out.

The best we can do is admire it
and soak up the sweet goodness
it freely provides to us all.

If we immerse ourselves in it,
we won't need bosses
'cause we will do the right thing naturally.

All the many things that flow from it
is what allows us to call it The Big Idea
and rest securely in that knowledge.

That security keeps us from making missteps.

Think of The Big Idea like gentle rain drops
flowing down the grassy hillsides into creeks,
streams and then rivers to gather together
and become a mighty ocean.

the man who can harness
and control his own self
is mighty

THIRTYTHREE

A fella who gets the best of other folks
may be strong.

But the man who can harness
and control his own self
is mighty.

And the cowpoke
with empty saddlebags
who is content with what he has got,
is just as rich as a cattle baron.

Keep your nerve,
stay on your horse
and you will make it
to the end of the trail.

Even if you die
you will not expire
and your spirit will endure.

THIRTYFOUR

Squint your eyes
and look across the prairie
to where the sun rises,
then turn and search the horizon
where it sets.

In both the east and west
and in between
you will find The Big Idea.

It gives rise to the land
but it does not take credit for creation.

All things come from it,
but it makes no claim on nothing.

As wide as the sky
and small as a grain of sand;
all things come from it and return to it,
but The Big Idea is the boss of none of it.

Which is why I call it great.

A good old boy is like that.

He doesn't think much of himself,
nor try to accomplish much
and consequentially
he is the image of greatness.

THIRTYFIVE

A good old boy
who hangs on to The Big Idea
will be sought after far and wide.

Folks who find him
will avoid calamity,
the sky will provide them shelter
and the earth restful repose.

Flibbertigibbets will traipse off
after saloon tunes and sweet treats.

Serious minded seekers
who find The Big Idea
will discover that it has
no taste at all,
not a dab of flavor.

When they try to examine it,
they can hardly see it
and listening
as closely as they can,
they will just hear silence.

But it will meet their every need
and it will never run dry.

a rock
can be
softer
than a
feather pillow

THIRTYSIX

You can't scrunch up
if you weren't stretched out to begin with.

And how would you know you were weak,
if you had not started out strong?

If you think that the herd
has become scattered
over all tarnation,
it is just because you know
they were corralled together afore hand.

Now this is how you come to understand
that a wet noodle can be
stronger than a steel chain
and a rock can be
softer than a feather pillow.

Just 'cause a fish
don't know it is wet,
is no reason to look for
a fish home on the prairie.

And an outfit that
is armed to the teeth
will do well to keep all its
six shooters and rifles
out of sight.

THIRTYSEVEN

The Big Idea
don't do nuthin' at all.

Yet everything gets done just the same.

If the politicians and big bosses understood this,
all the falderal would unfold without a hassle.

If they still felt compelled to make a show,
they could fall back on the nameless notions
that nobody knows and never forgets.

Don't slap a label on it
and nobody will want it.

When nobody wants it
nobody makes a fuss about it.

This is how everything
can come together
without a big commotion.

THIRTYEIGHT

Good old boy's noggins
are plumb full of The Big Idea.

They know to keep their traps shut
and never let it leak out for all of tarnation to see.

Good old boys keep the best and brightest
to their own self.
So they are fit to follow.

Wranglers who just know a little bit
about the Nature Trail,
will try to hog tie and hang on to
that which can not be grasped.

So they end up with just a general notion
of which way to mosey down the trail.

Cowhands that have never given the first thought
to The Big Idea, much less the Nature Trail,
will get the whole dang herd lost
while they pretend to be ace trackers.

You can keep quiet about what you know,
or you can talk about what you just forgot,
or you can pretend to lead
with what you have never possessed.

It all flows downhill.

Which is why the good old boy
picks up the mushroom
and not the cow-patty it is growing on.

Since the days of
my grand-pappy's grand-pappy,

The Big Idea is known
in all its ways as single and true

THIRTYNINE

Since the days of my grand-pappy's grand-pappy,
The Big Idea is known in all its ways as single and true.

The big blue up above is one sky from horizon to horizon.
The solid ground under yer' feet stays put in one place.
Yer' heart and soul move you as one mind.
And the beautiful valley is one welcoming place
for rivers, critters and cowpokes.

It is The Big Idea that shapes all the variance into a single life source.
This single truth is what makes
the big boss and the bigger bosses worth following.

If the sky were not receptive to the men and the mountains
that move up into it, the sky might crack.
If your mind is not single, you might lose your mind.
If the valley is not singly open to the free flow of water and life,
it could become a mud pit graveyard.

And the bosses will find themselves at the bottom of the heap,
pickin' up cow-patties if they forget The Big Idea.

This is why the good bosses always remember
they started as cowpokes.
And the highborn that know The Big Idea
walk among the common folk.

A wagon that gets taken apart into wheels and axels and sideboards
ain't a wagon no more.
Its single purpose has been undone.

When you get the true and single settled down into yer' gut,
you won't sparkle like diamonds,
but you won't be a dullard stepping stone neither.

FOURTY

Try to spot The Big Idea
and it will have just faded away
beyond the horizon.

Try to use The Big Idea
as a strong binding
and you will discover
that it is weaker than a wet noodle.

The Nature Trail
and all the countless notions
came from The Big Idea.

But The Big Idea
came from nothing.

So nothing
is really the foundation
of everything.

FOURTYONE

The seasoned trail hand
always cogitates on The Big Idea.

A fellow who has survived a few trips on the cattle drive
will remember The Big Idea occasionally.

But a greenhorn hears of The Big Idea,
then chuckles, snorts and guffaws.

Without a good laugh now and again,
I don't think it would be The Big Idea.

The sunny road seems shady.
The way ahead looks like what you left behind.

Easy going is a tough row to hoe.

The gilt of the glorious is tarnished.
The fullness of glory is empty.
Glory is a desert's mirage.

A prissy woman is worse than a saloon girl.
A square deal is shaped like a good egg.

The best fruit is not new and green.
The sweetest song is silent.
The most useful shape is no shape at all.

The Big Idea is not where you are looking for it,
nor named what you call it.

But without it,
you will never be full and fit.

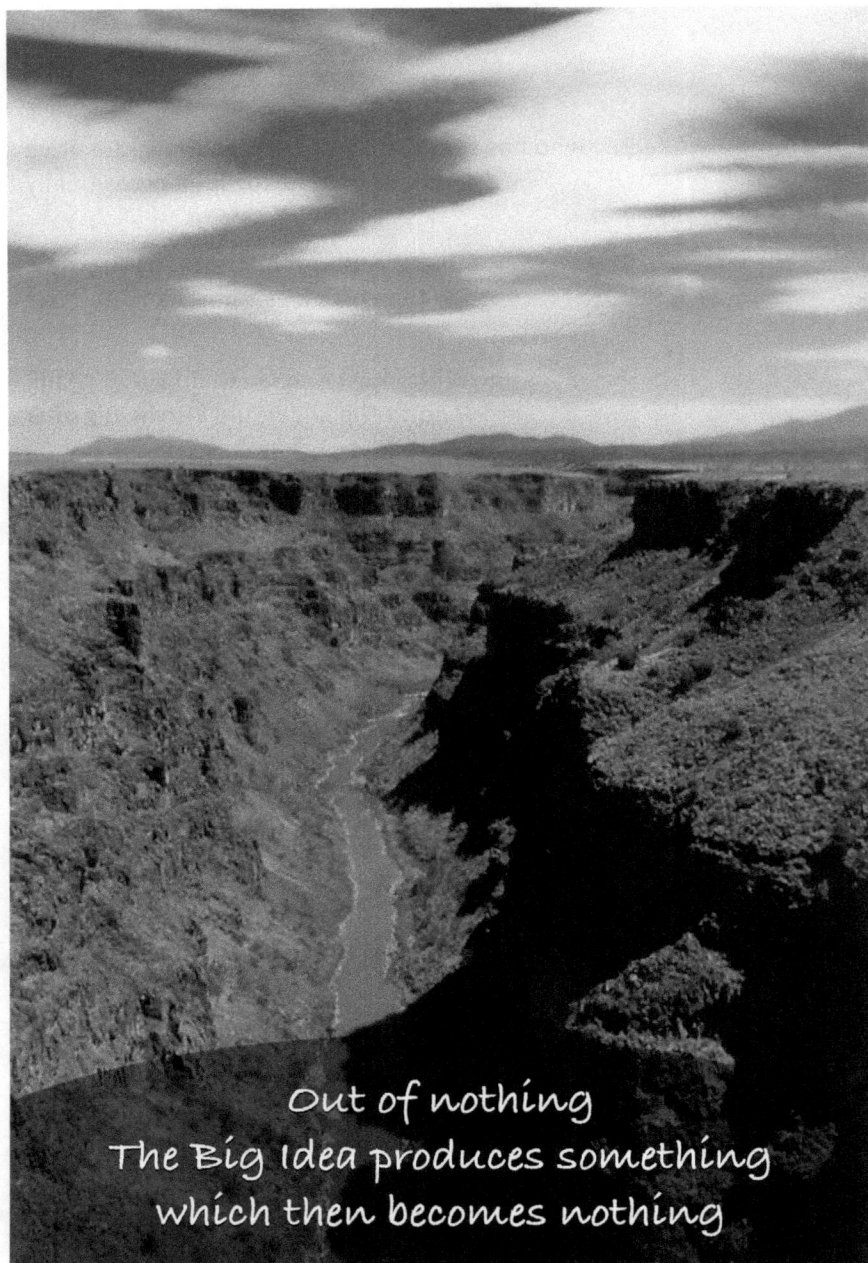

Out of nothing
The Big Idea produces something
which then becomes nothing

FOURTYTWO

Out of nothing
The Big Idea produces something
which then becomes nothing.

It is this nothing, something, nothing
that shows us a way called The Nature Trail.

All the things that ever was
and ever will be
came and went and came again
on this light and dark circle
of becoming and unbecoming.

City folk hate to think of being lone rider,
down and out tumbleweeds.

But those are just the names
a good old boy will choose for himself.

I ain't the first geezer to yammer these yarns.

Hard riding pistoleros
are rushing to an early grave.

Me, I'll stay low in the gravel gulch,
ride slow and become nothing in a natural way.

FOURTYTHREE

Soft and easy
always wins over
hard and unyielding.

The tightest locked doors
can't hold back
that which flows
and slips
through the cracks.

Just so, a good old boy
gets things done
without doing a thing.

He says all that needs
to be communicated
without uttering
a single word.

Soft and easy
always wins over
hard and unyielding

FOURTYFOUR

A buckaroo who is only bent
on making a name for himself
is the kind of fella
you'd just as soon forget.

He thinks his treasure
is in his bulging gold pouch
and never notices that he is flat busted
'cause he has an empty heart.

He shoots his wad at the General Store
on things he doesn't need, doesn't want and will soon forget.

He fills up his saddlebags with things he can't use,
and as night follows day, they are just things he will loose.

A good old boy ain't got much
and don't want much.

He is content
and he never runs out.

FOURTYFIVE

Pinpoint performance
appears to be amiss,
but it always hits
the target dead center.

The well stocked store shed
might look like it's empty,
but it will always
have what you need.

A straight fence line
is seen as curvy.

A great carpenter
will be called a
thumb busting doofus.

A powerful preacher
might be thought of as
a mumbling know-nothing.

Get a move-on to beat the cold.

Sit still and let the heat pass.

Clear headedness and single purpose
will see you true across all the earth and sky.

FOURTYSIX

When folks remember The Big Idea
their ponies will play and fertilize the pasture.

When The Big Idea is forgotten,
those ponies will turn into war horses crowding the road.

Craving is the worst sin.

Discontent is the worst misfortune.

Greed is the worst transgression.

That's why folk who are completely self sufficient
are content with their own contentment.

When folks remember
The Big Idea
their ponies will play
and fertilize the pasture

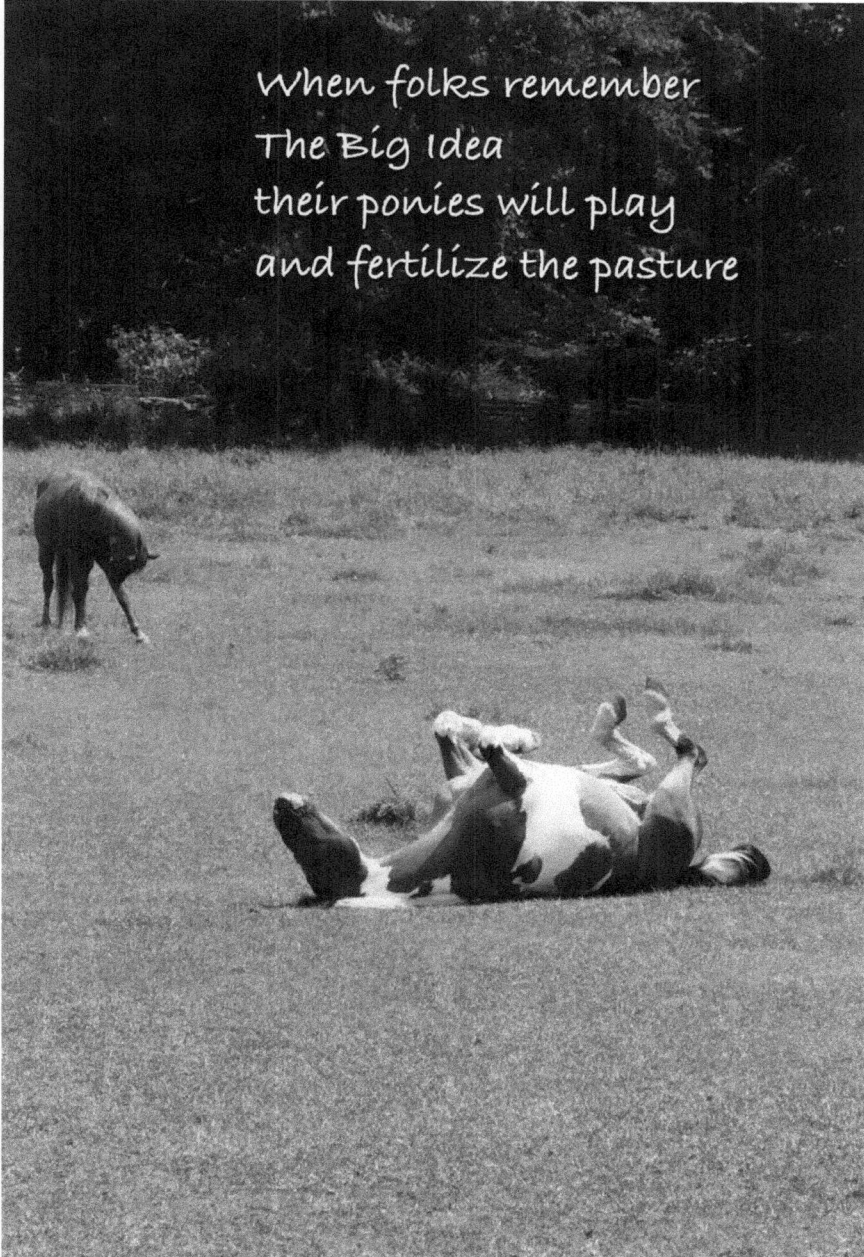

FOURTYSEVEN

A good old boy
doesn't have to head out the gate
to know where the Nature Trail goes.

And he doesn't have to look out the window
to understand the Big Idea in the sky.

Those that roam and search
don't know where they've been
nor understand what they've seen.

That's why a good old boy
can stay put and still know
the ways of the world.

He can explain the
"whys & wherefores"
without looking for the answers.

He never tries and
his work is accomplished
without effort.

FOURTYEIGHT

A fella who studies on
how to get ahead every day
is likely to become
the big-shot center of attention.

But a good old boy
who cogitates on the Big Idea,
is noticed less and less
until it seems like
he has plumb disappeared.

And when he has become nothing,
there is nothing he can't accomplish.

The good old boy never uses tricks
to win the day and lead the way.

The tricksters are losers
and not fit to be leaders.

FOURTYNINE

A good old boy's heart and mind
ain't wasted cogitating and fretting
about his own-self.

He gives his attention to other folks
and their hearts and minds.

When folks are good to him,
he gives them good back.

And when folks are bad to him,
he gives them good too.

So goodness is always his companion.

Anyone who greets him
with truth and honesty,
gets truth and honesty in return.

Those that lie and
try to cheat the good old boy,
are also given truth and honesty in return.

So truth and honesty
are spread across the land.

The good old boy lives a cautious life
and don't get distracted.

So folks pay attention to him.

He treats everyone
like they were his own children.

Anyone who greets him
with truth and honesty,
gets truth and
honesty in return.

Those that lie
and try to cheat
the good old boy,
are also given truth
and honesty in return

FIFTY

Every fella is born, lives and dies.

In an outfit of ten wranglers;
three boys are full of life,
three are busy with dying,
and three are living in ways that will just get them killed.

But one good old boy travels the trail and rides the range
without fear of mountain lions, angry bulls or bandits.

The lion's claws can't scratch him,
the bull's horns can't gouge him
and the bandit's bullets can't touch him.

Why is this so?

Because a good old boy on the Nature Trail
has no place in him for death to enter.

FIFTYONE

The Big Idea is where you come from
and the Nature Trail is how you get where you're going.

Where ever you wander in the wide world,
everyone you encounter owes their giddy-up and get-along
to the Big Idea and the Nature Trail.

No one is forced to tip their hat to the Big Idea
or sing praises of the Nature Trail,
it comes as natural as breathing in and breathing out.

The Big Idea is your birth momma,
and the Nature Trail is your wet nurse,
your schoolmarm, your best friend and your trail boss.

They give you all you've got and want nothing in return.

Why that is, is a mystery to us all.

FIFTYTWO

You can think of the Big Idea
as the mother of the world.

Just as you know your own Ma,
she always knows you.

Mind your Ma, keep your mouth shut
and you'll stay out of trouble.

Flap your gums and stick your nose in where it don't belong
and she will leave you to your self made misery.

If you look in the mirror and see just another nobody,
you're a pretty smart fella.

A tenderfoot outlasts the tough guys
and if he always remembers the Big Idea,
the Nature Trail will never fail him.

You can think of the Big Idea
as the mother of the world

Just as you know your own Ma,
she always knows you

FIFTYTHREE

Even a greenhorn
can follow the Big Idea.

But if he starts acting
too big for his britches,
he will have lost his way.

The Nature Trail
is straight, true
and easy to follow.

Folks that stray down the side roads
can count on getting lost.

When the ranch house is decorated
with expensive bric-a-brac and doodads,
the garden will be weedy and the barn empty.

Wearing fancy duds,
brandishing pearl handled revolvers,
stuffing a fat face and guzzling beer,
is the trademark of scalawags and outlaws.

It is contrary to the Big Idea.

FIFTYFOUR

A well sown crop
will take good root.

A well guarded grub stake
won't get pilfered.

Well raised progeny
will honor their grand pappy.

When a fella clings to the Big Idea,
he becomes a sign of the Nature Trail.

When his family follows forthwith,
they show its myriad paths.

The ranches they brand
will be filled with virtue.

And the whole countryside
will abide in the Big Idea.

The Nature Trail
leads from a fella, to his family,
to their outfits, and the land far and wide.

How do I know this?

'Cause it's the Big Idea!

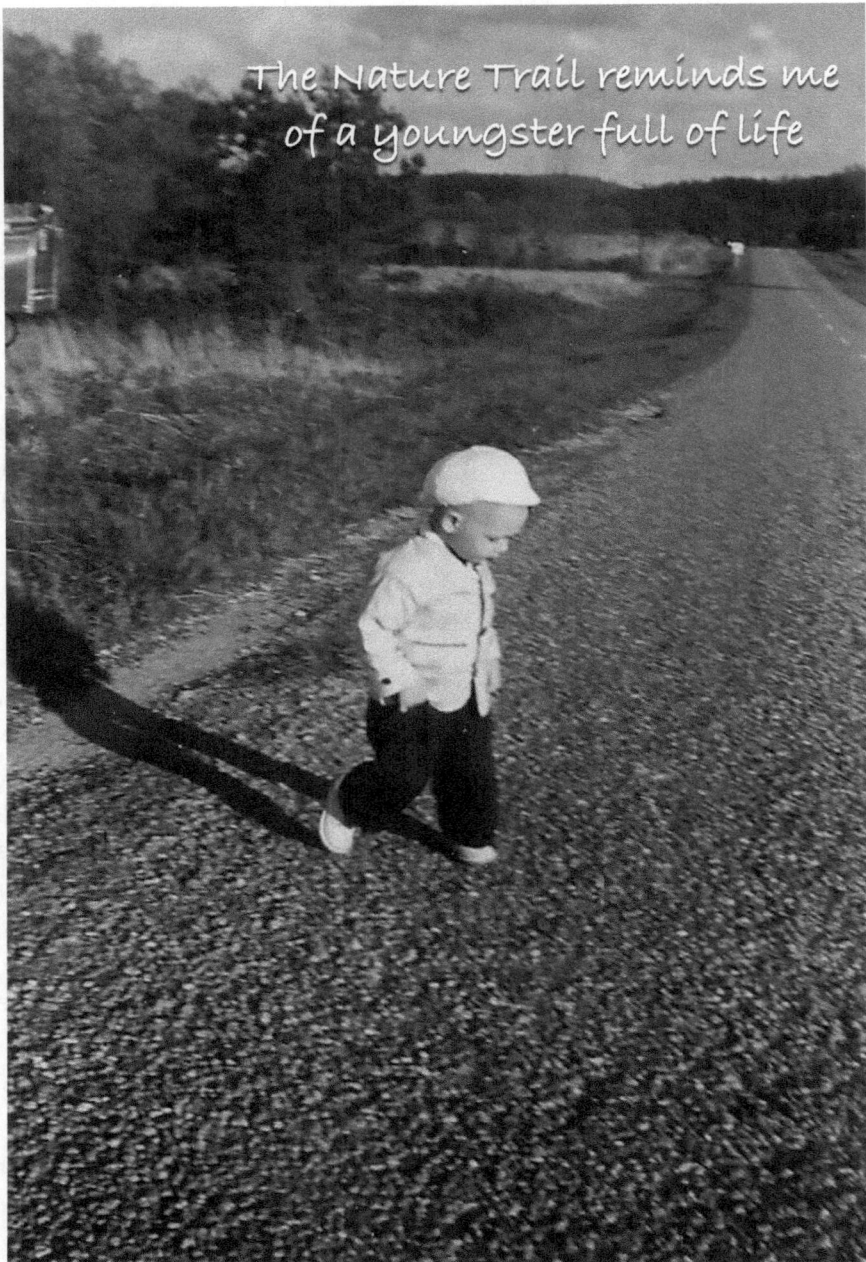

The Nature Trail reminds me
of a youngster full of life

FIFTYFIVE

The Nature Trail reminds me
of a youngster full of life.

A snake in the grass
can't bite the little feller,
a bear won't harm him
and an eagle would never snatch him away.

The child may have bendy bones and soft muscles,
but he has a firm grip all the same.

He hasn't learned nuthin' about the birds and the bees,
but his tallywhacker is strong and ready.

This boy can holler and cry all day long
and never get hoarse.

He is the perfect rip snorter.

This rip snorting child
reveals the ever lasting.

If you can see what I'm saying,
you'll know what you know.

Helping the child grow brings you blessing.
Seeing the power in his heart gives you strength.

It is foolish to waste your strength
and become decrepit.

Decrepit things are contrary to the Big Idea
and don't last very long.

How he embraces obscurity
is a puzzle within a mystery

FIFTYSIX

The fellas with the real answers
save their thoughts for themselves.

Unlike the gum flappers
who yammer on
about their own ignorance.

That's why a good old boy
will keep his mouth shut
and pay no attention to distractions.

He never seems too sharp
'cause dullness is his way.

When other folks
are tied up with confusion,
he just untangles the knots
without bringing attention to himself.

How he embraces obscurity
is a puzzle within a mystery.

The good old boy doesn't change
when people claim to love him
nor when they spit their hate.

When he makes a profit
or suffers a loss,
he doesn't seek praise
nor does he run from disgrace.

He is honored by all
'cause he seeks no honor.

FIFTYSEVEN

Run the ranch with righteousness.
Send in the cavalry by surprise.
Control the countryside by doing nothing.

How do I know these things?

Here's how:

Rule makers are wealth takers,
they keep folks poor.

When gizmos abound,
so does confusion.

And cleverness goes
hand in hand with foolishness.

Create more laws and you can be sure
you'll get more law breakers.

That's why the good old boy says:

"If I don't try to fix folks,
they'll fix themselves."

"If I keep my mouth shut,
they will make the right choices."

"If I sit still and stay out of the way,
people will prosper."

"If I don't want anything,
they will be satisfied."

Control the countryside
by doing nothing

FIFTYEIGHT

A trail boss who runs his outfit
with a light and easy hand
will have wranglers who are focused
and well functioning.

The boss holding his reigns tight
is going to find his fellas raucous and unruly.

Calamity follows good fortune
and the best of luck
will be preceded by misery.

There is no way to predict
when or in which order they appear.

Punishing evil
becomes an evil in itself.

This has bewildered folks
long as I can remember.

That's why a good old boy
will do good,
but is not a do-gooder.

He is straightforward in a round about way
 and he is the brightest when he seems to be in the dark.

FIFTYNINE

A wrangler who cares for the herd
and keeps straight with the trail boss
understands "waste not, want not".

He rises before the sun
and gathers what he needs for his work

There ain't nothing that comes up
he is not ready for,
nor challenge
he can not overcome.

The prepared buckaroo
knows no limits
and can be trusted
to be his own boss.

When he is walking,
his gait is firm and steady.

When he is riding,
he is sure in the saddle.

He is the very vision of
the Big Idea and the Nature Trail.

SIXTY

You can run a big outfit
with the same economy
you use for frying a little fish.

Skip the scaling and scraping.

Take an easy hand
and spare the falderal.

You will find that
the herd won't get spooked
and your wranglers
will have peace of mind.

Keep yer' noggin
on the Big Idea
and have an easy ride
down the Nature Trail.

Keep yer' noggin
on the Big Idea
and have an easy ride
down the Nature Trail

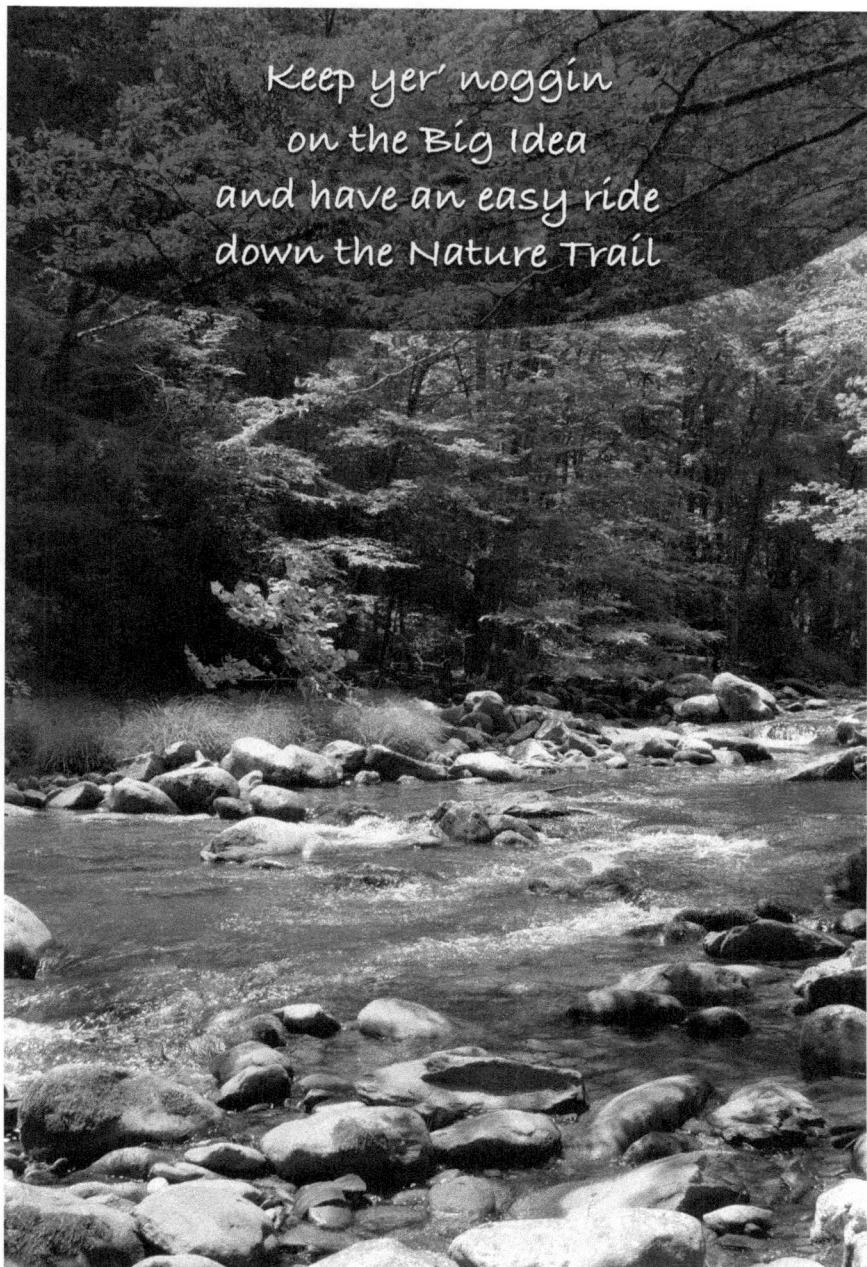

SIXTYONE

A passel of quiet wranglers
can be the glue that
sticks together the whole outfit.

A rancher's wife
might be mistaken
for just a frilly filly,
when in fact she is
the might and mettle
that holds the homestead.

It is the unassuming,
with the appearance of
meekness, mildness
and femininity
that contains
a great hidden strength
which serves us all.

she is the might and mettle
that holds the homestead

SIXTYTWO

The Big Idea
provides a good old boy
with a treasure trove.

Even an outlaw
it does not turn away.

Pretty talk
might sell a pig in a poke,
but straight talk
will make folks friends.

A trail boss
ain't doing his job
if he just runs off
the rascals and loafers.

Much better to
point them to the Big Idea
and show them the way
along the Nature Trail.

When bad men
become good old boys,
the herd is cared for
and the trail boss can rest easy.

SIXTYTHREE

Damn the dams!

Just go with the flow.

You'll learn how delicious
plain grub can be.

How an empty poke
can produce a big pay day.
And slim saddlebags
can provide all you need.

Don't respond
to a smart-mouth with a fist;
open your hand and offer friendship.

Plug the little leak
before it gushes
and tame your ponies
'afore they're big stallions.

The worst consternations
start as small annoyances.

That's why a good old boy
looks to the little things.

Don't promise what you can't deliver
nor bite off more than you can chew.

Take on tasks when they are doable
and in the end you'll find
you have nothing to do.

SIXTYFOUR

A stray steer resting in the shade is easy to lasso.
Trouble that is out of sight beyond the horizon is easy to avoid.

A weak willed pony is easy to break
and a small pack of coyotes is easy to run off.

Cogitate on your challenges before they challenge you,
and corral the herd before it can scatter.

A tree that you can't even reach around, began as a little sprig.
A hay stack as big as a barn, started off with a single bale.
And a trail drive across the great prairie begins with a single "giddy-up".

A fella who tries to fix that which don't need fixing,
is just going to break something.

When this fella gets all grabby, things will just slip through his fingers.

A good old boy knows to let things be and not hold on too tight.
He never falls on his face rushing for the end of the trail.
His last step is as sure as his first.

The best of the good old boys wants to want nothing,
cogitates on his ignorance,
is content in places where the town folk don't want to be.

All that travel the Nature Trail are aided by him
and he never gets in their way.

The best of the good old boys
wants to want nothing

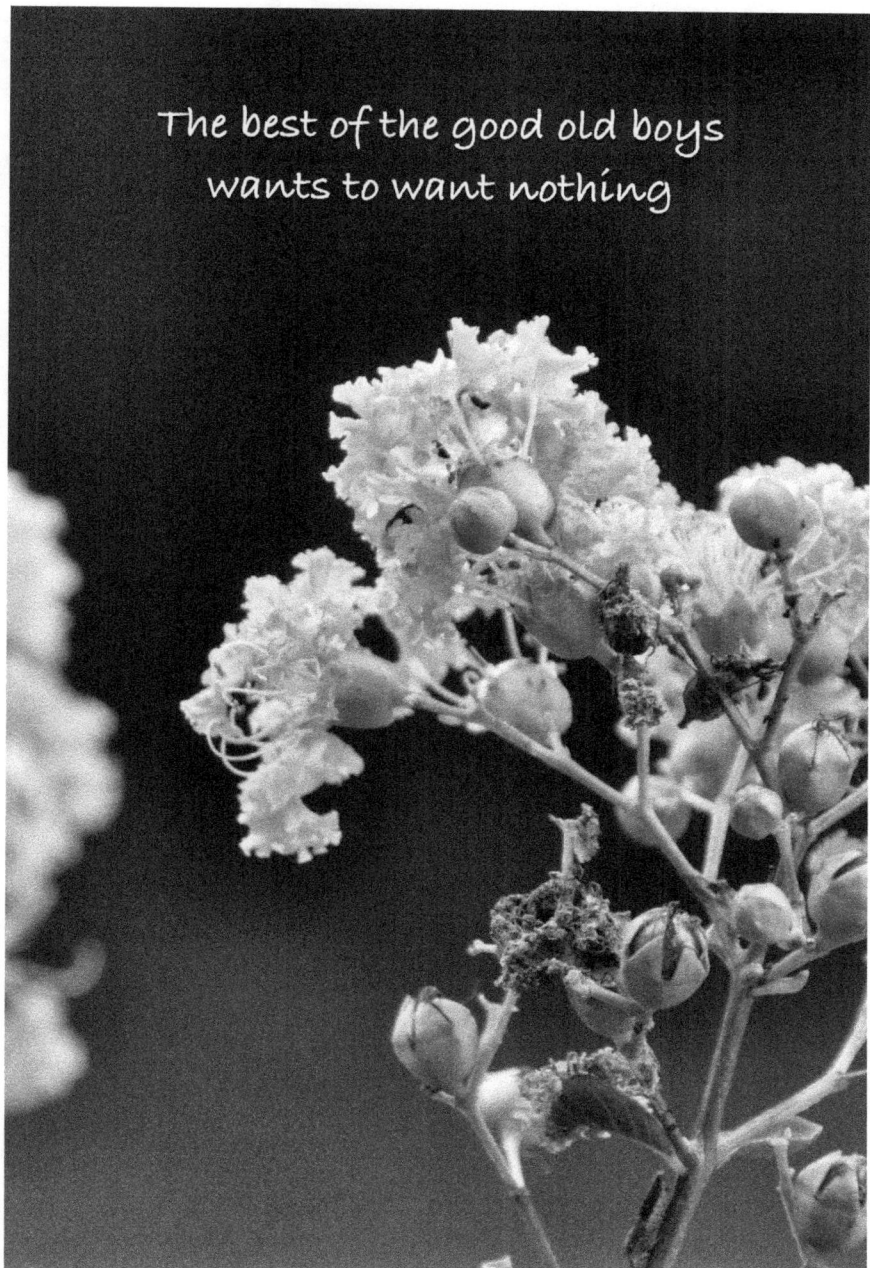

SIXTYFIVE

In my grand pappy's day
they knew it was better
to be know-nothings
than to be know-it-alls

A rowdy outfit
that won't follow orders
thinks they are smarter
than the trail boss.

The trail boss
is the head of the outfit
because he appreciates
his own ignorance.

The thing that makes
common sense so valuable
is that, it is just not that common.

SIXTYSIX

Whether your trail is through
the mountains or valleys,
every drop of water you see
is making its way on down to the river
and from there further down to the ocean.

The ocean is the chief of all the waters
because it occupies the lowest spot.

That's why the best trail boss
brings his outfit around
to his way of doing things
by laying low
and keeping out of sight.

He leads all the wranglers
but no one thinks of him as the boss.

He guides them through danger
and no one gets hurt.

Nobody fusses with him
'cause he don't fuss with nobody.

SIXTYSEVEN

Everybody makes a great fuss
about the Big Idea,
but there ain't nothing to it.

It is that "nothing"
which is the source of its greatness.

If a fella tries to show folks that he is a big shot,
he will just reveal himself as a pip-squeak.

The Big Idea has bequeathed us three treasures:
compassion, frugality and humility.

A compassionate fella
is fit to be chief of the brave.

Those who are frugal
can afford to be generous.

And the humble
can lead without tripping over their own egos.

Those foolish fellas who abandon
compassion, frugality and humility,
then try to be brave, generous leaders anyway,
are not long for this world.

On the the other hand,
compassion will lend to conquest
and the humble and frugal
can count on the help of heaven.

The Big Idea has bequeathed us
three treasures:
compassion, frugality and
humility

SIXTYEIGHT

The most successful
warriors, don't like war.

The best fighters
are not angry.

And the victorious
don't make a fuss
about winning.

A great leader
is a good follower.

This is called
the pride of the humble,
the abundance of poverty,
the clumsiness of grace.

Since my grand pappy
was a pea-pod,
it is the best way
of the good old boys.

SIXTYNINE

A great chief once said,
"I dare not start a battle.

Much better to be ready to defend.
I dare not ride forth, much better to retreat."

This is called:

Getting on along,
by laying low.

Scaring your enemy
with a friendly smile.

Winning the war
without firing a shot.

Catastrophe and calamity
comes from
disrespecting your enemy.
A sure fire way to lose your step.

When two outfits come to loggerheads,
it'll be the fellas who are best aware
of their own shortcomings
that will prevail.

SEVENTY

A good old boy talks straight
and gives directions
that are easy to follow.

But the city folk always act like they didn't hear him
and tromp around with no idea which way to go.

Straight talk
comes from a clear mind
and good directions
come from knowledge of the trail.

It is no surprise that empty headed know nothings
can't even begin to understand a good old boy.

The cow pokes who get it,
are few and far between.

They don't need to see the good old boy
in fancy duds swinging a gold pouch
to value his words.

Straight talk
comes from a clear mind
and good directions
come from knowledge of the trail.

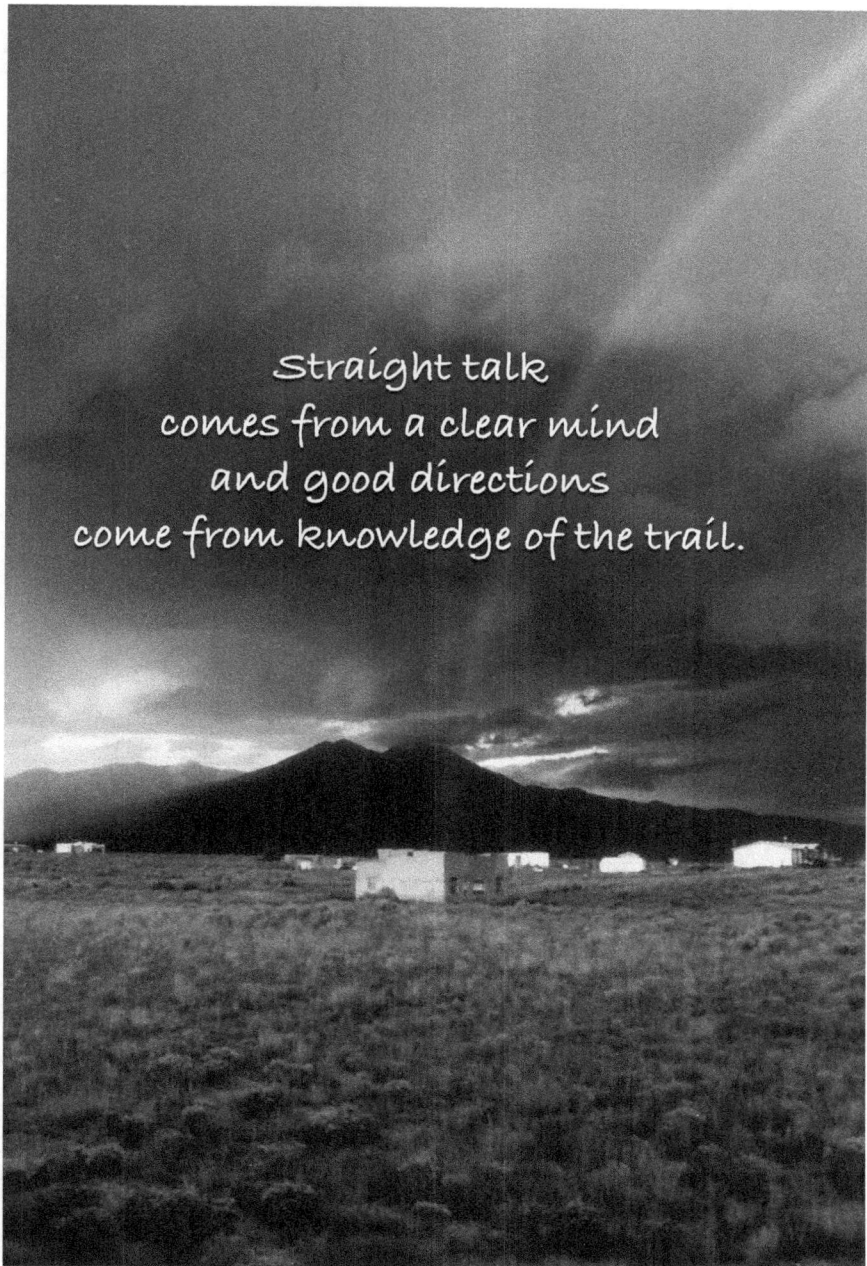

SEVENTYONE

A good old boy
embraces his own ignorance.

And the know-it-alls
are sick in the head!

It pains a good old boy
to even imagine that he
could ever be a know-it-all.

It is only 'cause
he is sick of that head sickness
that a good old boy is not sick.

SEVENTYTWO

Folks who are lackadaisical about grizzly bears
will end up as grizzly poop.

And those who indulge in feeling sorry for themselves
will have sorry lives.

Don't feel sorry
and you won't be sorry.

A good old boy knows all this,
but he keeps it to himself.

He cherishes his own heart
but makes no falderal of it.

This is how he is able
to choose substance over show.

SEVENTYTHREE

When a brave wrangler
charges right into the fray,
he will most likely get himself killed.

A brave wrangler who hangs back
and checks things out first,
usually gets to live for another rodeo.

Charging in or hanging back
can flip flop so that
sometimes either one
can be the right choice
or the wrong choice.

The Nature Trail is strewn
with these kinds of conundrums,
which is why a good old boy is serious
and cogitates in his choosing.

The Big Idea never competes,
yet it always wins.

It is silent,
but always tells you
what you need to know.

It never calls you,
but you always come.

The loop of its lasso is wide,
woo wee, and it never misses.

The loop of its lasso is wide,
woo wee, and it never misses

SEVENTYFOUR

Fearless folk
ain't got no respect for the grave.

But if you scare them just right,
it could help them avoid
the hang man's noose.

Now, I don't mean
you should grab
a hammer and saw
and start building a gallows.

Go that route
and you're more likely
to cut off your own thumb.

Show some caution,
no need to interfere.

SEVENTYFIVE

Folk will end up hungry
when the mayor and marshal
take too much for taxes.

And the town bosses
will have a heck of a time
running things
if they meddle too much
in the town folk's affairs.

They all flit and gallivant
like they've completely forgotten
that pine box waiting for them
at the end of their trail.

Too much involvement
in every day fickle affairs
makes for a shallow life
followed by a shallow grave.

It's much better
to stay disengaged.

SEVENTYSIX

When we are born,
we are soft, weak and flexible.

At the end of the trail,
we are tough, stiff and brittle.

Even a great tree
starts as a supple sapling.

The green grass that
soothes and caresses
your tootsies,
will turn brown
and crunchy in the end.

Death is hard and brittle.

Softness and flexibility
are the signs of life.

This is why the best wranglers
hang back and avoid conflict.

A big strong tree
with its limbs stretched out wide,
is just inviting
the lumberjacks to their work.

If you want to stay above ground,
it's best to give in and go with the flow.

SEVENTYSEVEN

Big Idea and the Nature Trail
can be compared to
bending an archer's bow.

When the string comes back,
the top goes down
and the bottom comes up.

It is only natural
for them that has plenty to give
and those that have little to receive.

But it's not that way for city folks.

They take from the poor
and give to the rich.

Can you show me a fella
with fat money bags
who is making the world
a better place?

I think not!

A good old boy
gets things done and
don't take no credit for it.

And if you thank him
and slap him on the back,
he won't smile nor frown.

He just goes on about his business.

there is nothing better than water
for making mountains into valleys
and washing away anything
that is hard and unyielding

SEVENTYEIGHT

There ain't nothing softer
and more receptive than water.

And just the same,
there is nothing better than water
for making mountains into valleys
and washing away anything
that is hard and unyielding.

The Big Idea makes clear
that the weak beats the strong
and the flexible
is more enduring than the stiff.

But nobody manages
to walk that talk.

That's why the good old boy says
scalawags are filling the pulpits
and crooked politicians
are getting all the votes.

It's hard to grasp
the truth in a contradiction.

SEVENTYNINE

When a feud is settled,
bad blood and a grudge is sure to follow.

So a good old boy
will always keep his side of a bargain,
without pushing the other fella to do the same.

The Nature Trail is free for both sides to travel,
but it is the good old boy who understands
that it is the only way he can go.

EIGHTY

There's a town out on the prairie
where the marshal and the mayor
ain't so bossy.

Folks there don't want to die,
but they don't run from it neither.

They have fancy buggies and fine saddles,
but you never see folks riding around.

The town has plenty of revolvers and rifles,
but no one has occasion to shoot them.

They don't go in for new fangled gadgets,
they think their food is just fine
without sauce or gravy.

And they never dress like peacocks.

From time to time they hear dogs barking
and roosters crowing down the road,
but it never occurs to them
to go gallivanting after the noises.

They are content
where they are,
with what they've got,
doing what they have always been doing.

The nature trail will lead you
to all you need

and the good old boys
understand you don't have to
rush to get there.

EIGHTYONE

Syrupy words are not sweet
and the truth is not music to your ears.

A good cowpoke don't quarrel
and quarrelers don't make good cowpokes.

Know-it-alls ain't got a dab of sense
and the real smart fellas
appreciate their own ignorance.

The best of the good old boys
don't fill the store shed
for his own self.

He takes care of the whole outfit
and finds he has all he needs as well.

The nature trail will lead you
to all you need
and the good old boys
understand you don't have to
rush to get there.

ABOUT THE AUTHOR

Geezer is a self educated old man.
Still happily stubbing his toes in the dark.

Writing, typography
and shutter bugging
by Jimmy Tucker.

Proofing and muse services
by Laura Floyd Tucker

RebelTao.com

TuckerCreative.org

CoastCommons.com

TuckerCreative.SmugMug.com

www.ingramcontent.com/pod-product-compliance
Lightning Source LLC
Chambersburg PA
CBHW071637050426
42443CB00026B/682